The Dietitian's Resupply Box

A Guide to Thru-Hiking on a Plant-Based Diet

Anna Herby, MS, RD

Disclaimer

The nutritional information found here is not intended to take the place of professional medical advice, diagnosis, or treatment. Always seek advice of your physician or other qualified health provider with any questions you may have regarding a medical condition. Please do not disregard professional medical advice or delay seeking it because of something you have read in this book.

The following is intended simply as information and ideas about how to eat healthy on the trail. This guide is not intended to convince anyone to go vegan, or to say that one must follow a plant-based diet in order to successfully complete a thru-hike. Each hiker can draw her own conclusions about what to eat, how certain foods make her feel, and what works best based on personal habits and preferences.

To further clarify the intention of this book, here are a couple helpful definitions:

Thru-hiker: An individual who sets out to hike a trail from one point to another over the course of days, weeks, or months.

Plant-based diet: A way of eating that focuses on whole plant foods such as whole grains, legumes, fruits, vegetables, nuts, and seeds, while minimizing or eliminating animal foods such as meat, fish, eggs, and dairy.

Table of Contents

Chapter One: The Benefits of Eating Plants

When it comes to nutrition, the average thru-hiker generally has one thing on his mind: calories. This is a valid concern for a person walking over 20 miles per day for months at a time with a 15- to 30-pound pack on his back. However, not all calories are created equal.

Many high-calorie foods like potato chips, ramen, beef jerky, candy bars, and ice cream are very low in nutrients. Eating processed snacks and foods high on the food chain (in other words, animal products) puts additional strain on your body to break down unnatural substances and detoxify your system. On top of the incredible demand of hiking marathon distances day after day, a poor diet can be just another challenge for your body to deal with. You don't just need calories, but also nutrients.

The Tarahumara Indians are perhaps the most similar model to the thru-hiker lifestyle. In a culture where running anywhere between 200 and 400 miles without stopping is a regular occurrence, these folks have their diet figured out.[1] Their fuel consists primarily of corn, beans, and chia seeds. Their diet is high in complex carbohydrates and very low in fat and cholesterol, yet they still get enough calories and protein to run for days on end. Though the Tarahumara people do eat meat on occasion, it is not a fundamental element of their diet.[2, 3]

It may also be helpful to look at the diet of some of the greats in the world of endurance athletes:

- In 2015, ultrarunner Scott Jurek accomplished the fastest known time for a supported hike of the Appalachian Trail. Jurek averaged over 50 miles per day and did it all on a plant-based diet.
- Venus and Serena Williams fuel their champion tennis career on a plant-based diet
- Rich Roll is a triathlete who completed five Ironman races in a row on a plant-based diet
- Current NFL stars Aaron Rodgers and Tom Brady follow plant heavy diet
- Marathon runner Fiona Oakes, body builder Jahina Malik, racecar driver Leilani Munter, former NFL star David Carter, and countless others are reaping the benefits of a plant-based diet for athletic performance

Knowing this diet works for Tarahumara Indians, professional athletes, and supported speed records is one thing. But how does this diet apply to the average thru-hiker who depends on resupply boxes and small grocery stores in mountain towns? Everything you eat, you carry on your back—meaning green smoothies are out and dehydrated noodles are in.

***

Let's go over just a bit of the research that helps explain why a diet high in plant foods is beneficial to the long-distance hiker. One of the main benefits reaped by vegan hikers is an increased recovery time, meaning less soreness after exercise. This is attributed, in part, to a higher intake of antioxidants and anti-inflammatory nutrients found in plant foods.

Any athlete who makes the switch from an omnivorous diet to a plant-based diet will tell you that the first benefit they notice is faster recovery. Whenever you put a strain on your body by exercising, tiny micro-tears occur in the fibers of your muscles. In addition, the act of exercising causes free radicals (damaged molecules) to form, which then go on to cause oxidative stress, injuring proteins, enzymes, and sometimes DNA. The combination of micro-tears and oxidative stress can lead to muscle soreness that lasts for days after the event.

One key to combating the damage of strenuous activity is eating foods high in antioxidants. These plant chemicals quench free radicals and help repair torn muscle fibers. For example, berries are extremely high in antioxidants. Studies show that cherries and blueberries can decrease muscle soreness in athletes by reducing inflammation.[4, 5]

Antioxidants are also found in other fruits (apples, berries, oranges, etc.), vegetables (broccoli, cabbage, beets, carrots, etc.), whole grains (brown rice, oats, whole wheat, etc.), and legumes (beans, peas, lentils, etc.). Their primary purpose is to protect plant cells from damage. Fortunately, they also help protect human cells. The more of these foods we have in our diet, the less likely we are to experience soreness and injury.

In addition to being able to quench free radicals, plant foods also have an anti-inflammatory effect on the body. A certain amount of inflammation happens after straining the body with any kind of exercise. When this exercise is hiking for hours on end, day after day, inflammation is inevitable. Perhaps the two most powerful things you can do to help your body deal with this stress are to rest adequately and eat a diet high in plant foods.

When vegan and vegetarian diets were put to the test against pesco-vegetarian and omnivorous diets, people following a vegan or vegetarian diet showed lower levels of inflammation.[6] Further studies have shown that even just cutting down on red meat can lead to lower levels of inflammatory markers in the blood.[7] This means that the specific compounds in the body that cause swelling, pain, aches, and redness are lower in vegans and vegetarians. These benefits can't be attributed to any one vitamin or mineral, but are noticed most profoundly when the balance of foods shifts away from animal foods and more toward plants.

Another strategy to decrease inflammation in the body is to avoid foods that specifically cause inflammation. Excess animal protein and fat has been shown to be inflammatory. While some inflammation in the body is necessary, too much can be detrimental. Researchers speculate that excess inflammation is due to a particular kind of fat that is found in animal foods: arachidonic acid. This is the exact material the body uses to make inflammatory molecules that, in excess, lead to aches and pains.[8] In other words, when you give your body more of the ingredients (animal fat) to make harmful substances (inflammation), it will. If you give your body more of the ingredients (plant foods) to make helpful substances (anti-inflammatory compounds), it will.[9]

Whether it is through speeding recovery, reducing inflammation, or simply providing fuel that is easier for the body to assimilate, plants work wonders for the endurance athlete and the thru-hiker alike.

Chapter Two: Macronutrients

There are two main categories of nutrients:

- Macronutrients: those needed in large quantities. This includes protein, carbohydrates, and fats.
- Micronutrients: those needed in small quantities. This includes vitamins, minerals, and other bioactive compounds (plant chemicals that effect a living organism, tissue or cell)

In this chapter we'll go over the basics of macro-nutrients, starting with protein.

Protein

There is much confusion in the health world about the importance of protein. Ever since its discovery in 1839, protein has taken center stage as one of the most sacred of nutrients. The word has its roots in the Greek word *proteos,* meaning *of most importance.* It is a vital component of our bodies and functions as a building block for muscles, organs, hormones, and all other functional parts of the body.

In the 19th century, protein was synonymous with meat, a cultural association that has stayed with us over the years. Having meat on the table was traditionally a sign of wealth and good health. As a result of the cultural bias toward meat and protein and the idea that more must always be better, the scientific recommendation for protein was set at twice the established amount needed to sustain the human body.[10]

That is the historical ground on which many people and health professionals still stand regarding their perspectives on nutrition. But if we take a step back, we start to see that there may be a different story. Healthy populations in Asia, South America, and Africa, for example, consume a diet very low in animal protein and have chronic disease rates that are a fraction of those in the Western world, meaning heart disease, diabetes, obesity, etc. is a rare occurrence.[11]

We know now that the full spectrum of amino acids, which proteins are made up of, can be found in every plant food. The idea that certain foods need to be combined with others in order to provide complimentary amino acid profiles, or a complete protein, has recently been discredited. For example, common wisdom dictates that beans must be eaten with rice in order to get all the essential amino acids in one meal. But recent studies show that your body will hold onto the amino acids it needs from the beans you ate last night and then take what else it needs from the rice you're having this afternoon. This means that you will absorb the amino acids that you need throughout the day or week without having to worry about combining proteins at a meal.[12, 13]

In the United States, the Recommended Daily Allowance of protein for a healthy adult is 0.8 grams per kilogram of body weight. For a woman who weighs 60 kilograms (132 pounds), this comes out to be 48 grams of protein; for a man who weighs 70 kilograms (154 pounds), 56 grams. Assuming a 2,000 calorie diet and 4 calories per gram of protein, this corresponds to about 11 percent of total calories from protein, or 9 percent of a 2,500 calorie diet. To round it off, the recommended amount was set at 10 percent (0.8 grams per kilogram) of calories from protein. This number has now been reviewed 14 times by a panel of expert scientists.[14] Given that a potato is 8 percent protein, throw in a half cup of beans at 27 percent protein, and we can easily meet or exceed our recommended protein needs on plant foods.

By including too much animal protein and increasing intake to the 17 percent (or more) of calories found in the standard American diet, we risk stressing the kidneys and liver in processing the high amounts of nitrogen. We also put ourselves at risk of, first, the adverse effects of animal protein itself and, second, displacing the health benefits of nutrient-rich plant foods.[15]

So how much protein do you need as a thru-hiker? According to the Academy of Nutrition and Dietetics, Dietitians of Canada, and the American College of Sports Medicine, endurance athletes need between 1.2 and 1.4 grams per kilogram of body weight per day.

So an endurance athlete weighing 132 pounds (60 kilograms) needs between 72 and 84 grams of protein per day. Let's assume this person is a thru-hiker and eats an impressive 4,000 calories in one day and only 10 percent of those came from protein. This still amounts to 400 calories of protein, or 100 grams (at 4 calories per gram), exceeding the recommended 84 grams. However, if this person were to not meet their calorie needs and only consume 2500 calories, they might end up with only 62.5 grams of protein (2500 calories x .10 = 250 calories from protein, 250 calories /4 calories per gram = 62.5 grams of protein).

Given that most plant foods are at least 10 percent protein and that nuts, seeds, and beans are even more, eating a diet of 10 percent protein (or even slightly higher) is completely manageable without eating meat. In the next chapter, you will see a daily breakdown of plant foods that meets or exceeds this recommendation. Note that the meal plan is based on a 4,000 calorie daily intake and exceeds protein needs of a 132-pound hiker. So even if you consume closer to 3000-3500 calories you are still likely to meet your basic protein needs, depending on your size.

Pro Tip: A common problem among thru-hikers is not getting enough calories and subsequently not getting enough protein. Though it is not necessary for everyone to drink a protein shake while thru-hiking, it may be helpful to some people. If you find yourself feeling week and tired, try having a plant-based protein drink before going to sleep. If it helps, keep doing it. If not, don't waste your money. You probably just need to eat more. When choosing a protein powder, try to avoid cheap proteins like soy protein isolate, whey, or casein. Pea and rice proteins are good, clean sources and are easily found in powder form. Some good brands include Vega, MRM Veggie, Sunwarrior, SAN RawFusion, NutraFusion, Orgain and Garden of Life.

Carbohydrates

Carbohydrates are of primary importance for thru-hikers since they provide energy. Through the digestive process, the body breaks down carbohydrates into sugar, or *glucose.* Glucose is the preferred source of energy for every muscle cell in the body as well as for your brain and organs. Glucose is so important that the body keeps a backup supply, just in case you don't get enough through food. This backup is called *glycogen* and is found in the muscles and liver. For example, when you're hiking but haven't eaten in a few hours, your body is making sugar to feed your muscles by burning glycogen. Many athletes and hikers are familiar with the *bonk* that occurs when you just can't go any further. This is due to running through all your glycogen storage until there is no more stored sugar left to feed the cells. The idea of carb-loading before an endurance event stems from the need to enable maximum glycogen storage in the liver and muscles to put off the *bonk* for as long as possible.

Carbohydrates can be found in foods such as grains, starchy vegetables, legumes, fruits, and sugary foods. Simple carbohydrates are those that the body can break down and turn into sugar very easily. This includes refined grains (such as bagels, tortillas, white rice, ramen, crackers, and instant oats), sweets like candy, fruit and dried fruit, (although fruit can also be considered a complex carbohydrate due to its fiber content). These foods are ideal for moments when you need a fast burst of energy—like the last couple of miles of a big climb or when you feel a little light-headed (or grumpy) from not eating for a while.

Complex carbohydrates take longer for the body to break down and provide a more slow-burning source of energy. Complex carbohydrates include whole grains (such as rolled oats, whole wheat tortillas/bread, and brown rice), legumes (such as lentils, beans, peas, and chickpeas), and starchy vegetables (such as potatoes and squash). These foods are good to eat at meals throughout the day to ensure a steady supply of energy and to keep you from becoming hungry right away. For a thru-hiker, a steady intake of both simple and complex carbohydrates throughout the day is ideal.

Fat

The most important thing about fats to a thru-hiker is that they provide over twice as many calories as carbohydrates or protein. One gram of fat provides 9 calories while 1 gram of carbohydrate or protein provides only 4 calories. However, not all fats are the same. Some fats, like saturated fat and cholesterol from animal-based foods, can be damaging to the blood vessels and increase a person's risk for disease.[16]

Omega-3 fatty acids are fats that the body uses to make anti-inflammatory compounds. While fish oil is one of the most bio-available sources of omega-3s, it can also be a highly concentrated source of toxins. There is also no evidence to support fish oil as protective against heart disease, as was once thought.[17] In a plant-based diet, one can get plenty of omega-3s through foods such as walnuts, ground flax seeds and chia seeds.

Although they do provide dense calories, fats are more work for the body to digest and, like protein, stay in the stomach for longer. This is good to keep us feeling full but can also be taken too far and make us feel bloated or sluggish. Studies have actually shown that immediately after eating a high-fat meal, fat enters the blood and slows down circulation.[18,19] This is not ideal during a long day of hiking. So, for hikers to take full advantage of this high-calorie nutrient, it's best to incorporate small amounts throughout the day in the form of nuts or added oil. To prevent digestive troubles, higher-fat meals should be eaten in the evening when you don't plan to hike anymore or when you are resting in town.

Calories

Getting enough calories is, for many people, the most challenging part about nutrition on the trail. It's nearly unavoidable to lose weight while hiking long distances for weeks on end, and this is okay. The concern comes when you feel constantly tired. This may be a sign of not getting enough calories. The simple solution is to take days off and eat as much as you can. Another solution may be to increase the amount of food you eat if you aren't already taking in your maximum amount of food.

When it comes to the question of how many calories you actually need for a day of hiking, the answer depends on many factors. It will vary depending on your own metabolism, the weight of your pack, the miles that you walk and the elevation change involved. Though not based on any hard science, a good rule of thumb is to account for 150 to 200 calories per mile. For a 20-mile day, this would be between 3,000 and 4,000 calories. Some may argue that even more calories are needed. And of course, the longer you're out on the trail, the more important it becomes to get enough calories.

Chapter Three: Micronutrients

Though micronutrients are only needed in small quantities, they are just as important as macronutrients. These tiny nutrients are found in whole plant foods by varying amounts. They include vitamins, minerals, and phytonutrients (beneficial plant-chemicals), and they serve as helpers (cofactors) in certain reactions. Phytochemicals are also responsible for the anti-inflammatory and antioxidant properties mentioned in chapter one.

While the functions of vitamins and minerals are generally well established, the benefits of phytonutrients is a growing area of study. Some phytonutrients you may have heard of include flavonoids, isoflavones, carotenoids and polyphenols. Currently, more than 8,000 phytochemical substances have been isolated from various fruits and vegetables, but we know that there are even more yet to be identified. These chemicals have been researched for everything from cancer prevention to anti-inflammatory properties, and are said to be one of the primary reasons a plant-based diet is so beneficial.[20]

The best way to get enough of these nutrients is to pack plenty of fruits, vegetables, whole grains and legumes in your resupply boxes.

In addition to the infamous "where do you get your protein?" question, those considering a plant-based diet may have concerns about getting enough of certain vitamins and minerals. Calcium, iron and B vitamins are a few that come up often. Electrolytes, while not specific to the plant-based diet, are another micronutrient necessary for any endurance athlete, and will also be addressed below.

Calcium

Calcium is one of the most abundant minerals in the human body and is essential for strong bones and teeth. Calcium also plays an important role in nerve function. Although most people associate calcium with dairy products, there is plenty of calcium to be found in plant foods such as almonds, beans, dried fruit and green vegetables. In fact, studies have found that those consuming enough calcium through plant sources are at no greater risk of bone fracture than those who get calcium through dairy.[21] Bone fractures are actually more common in women who drink milk regularly.[22] The higher amount of animal protein consumed, the more calcium is needed. So through decreasing meat and increasing beans, nuts and green vegetables, a person can meet or exceed their daily calcium needs on a plant-based diet.

Iron

Iron is a key mineral in blood cells and plays an important role in transporting oxygen throughout the body. This becomes important for endurance athletes and long distance hikers, especially at higher elevations, since these athletes are constantly circulating extra oxygen to their muscles. It is easy to meet daily iron needs through plant foods such beans, green vegetables, dried fruit, nuts and molasses. Additionally, vitamin C helps to facilitate iron absorption, and is plentiful in a plant-based diet (found in apples, oranges, tomatoes, bell peppers, etc.). Common wisdom dictates that heme-iron (found in animal foods) is better than non-heme iron (found in plant foods). While it's true that heme-iron is more easily absorbed by the body, it can have a pro-oxidant effect and cause free radical damage in the body.

When a person does not get enough dietary iron, she might feel sluggish and have low energy. On a long-distance hike, it may be hard to differentiate general fatigue from hiking 20+ miles per day versus fatigue from low iron. If you think you may be low on iron, try eating more beans, green vegetables, molasses and vitamin C-containing foods. Avoid dairy and caffeine, as these can impede iron absorption. If you still feel sluggish, have your blood levels tested. Only take an iron supplement if it is recommended by a doctor.

B Vitamins

Other nutrients to consider for optimal energy are B vitamins. These are nutrients that help with the function of the heart, red blood cells, nerves and the brain. The majority of B vitamins can be found in whole grains, legumes, nuts and seeds. Vitamin B12 is the one exception. This vitamin is actually a byproduct of bacteria. Omnivores get vitamin B12 from eating animals, but the animals get the nutrient from living close to dirt and bacteria. Since we generally live in a sanitized world and drink clean water, it is recommended to take a B12 supplement or eat fortified foods. Clif Bars, Luna Bars, some brands of nutritional yeast, and many other common hiker foods generally are fortified with B12.

Electrolytes

Electrolytes can be nutrients of concern for all endurance athletes, no matter what diet they follow. Sodium, potassium, magnesium and calcium are the main electrolytes that help to regulate fluid balance. During long bouts of exercise, these nutrients can be lost through sweat and may need to be replaced. Generally, a person can get enough electrolytes through the food he eats. However, if exercising for more than a few hours (or hiking all day), it can be a good idea to have an electrolyte drink such as Nuun or Gatorade. I've found the best time to drop some electrolyte powder into my water is in the afternoon, especially if it is hot, humid, or I'm climbing a hill.

Pro Tip: Needless to say, hydration plays a key role in long-distance hiking. Water is necessary for nearly every function in your body, so drinking enough will keep you on track for a long day. Keeping adequately hydrated will also help with muscle recovery and energy production. If you notice you have not peed in a while, or that your urine is a dark color, that is a sign that you may need to drink more water.

Other Supplements

Supplements such as turmeric, bromelain, or ginger may be helpful to further decrease inflammation. Ideally these things are incorporated into the diet, but if you are nursing an injury, supplementing with these substances can be helpful. These supplements can generally be found online or at a health food store.

Lastly, many people find that they have digestive problems on a hike. This issue is common in endurance runners and hikers alike, since our intestines are constantly bouncing up and down all day. Another reason for digestive upset is lack of fiber in the diet. Try increasing the amount of dried fruit, vegetables, whole grains, and beans in your diet. If that doesn't work, a shelf-stable probiotic might be helpful to help maintain healthy gut flora. Look for the kind that doesn't need to be refrigerated since you will be carrying it with you.

Chapter Four: Meal Planning for Long Hikes

With a basic understanding of how food works in the body and the benefits of eating plants, let's consider how this translates into the food you pack for a thru-hike.

Breakfast

Some hikers will wake up, pack their things, and then sit down for a warm bowl of oatmeal. Others prefer breakfast in bed. Still other hikers will immediately start walking after getting packed and begin their day with an energy bar rather than a meal. However the timing works, it's always a good idea to have some sort of intentional meal within two hours of when you first start walking.

Breakfast should consist of a hefty portion of carbohydrates with some fat and protein thrown in for good measure. Focusing on carbohydrates early in the day will help replenish your glycogen storage after not eating all night. The energy storage in your liver and muscles will get used up while you sleep. Since that energy is sourced from sugar, eating carbohydrates is the best way to replenish it.

Many hikers enjoy instant oatmeal for breakfast but then feel hungry again in an hour or less. This happens because there is very little fat, fiber and protein included in instant oatmeal packets. Fat helps to add calories, while protein helps to keep you feeling full for longer. Another reason instant oatmeal burns off so fast is that it is the most processed form of oats. This means that most of the fiber is stripped away. Fiber helps slow the digestion process and allow carbohydrates to burn more slowly.

Pro Tip: To make your breakfast last longer, try switching to regular rolled oats, or mix rolled oats with quick oats. They can be either cold-hydrated or eaten hot. Then add nuts, seeds, and dried fruit to balance the meal.

Lunch

It's always good to take a break in the middle of the day to refuel. Lunch can be one of the most flexible meals of the day. But just like breakfast, it should be relatively high in carbohydrates. Since you are not done walking for the day, your muscles need as much direct energy as they can get. A high-protein lunch will be hard for your body to process and may leave you feeling even more tired than before you ate. The goal for lunch should be to get in as many calories as possible without being so full that you need to take a nap. Some hikers can handle a heavier lunch, while others want to keep it light.

Pro Tip: It's always a good idea to include something that resembles fresh food in your lunch. For example, add some dried fruit to your peanut butter tortilla, or include homemade dried veggies in your ramen. This will boost the nutritional value of the meal and help increase fiber, which keeps you full longer.

Snacks

Let's be honest: the majority of a thru-hiker's calories are going to come from snacks. It's a good idea to keep a constant stream of calories coming in while you're hiking, and this means snacking a lot. At first, you may want to set an alarm to go off every one to two hours to remind you to eat a snack. After a while you'll get to know your body. Pay attention to what happens right before you start to feel hungry. Do thoughts of food randomly float into your mind? Is there just the slightest twinge in your stomach? Do you start to get frustrated easily? That's the time to eat a snack. Don't wait until you get so hungry that your blood sugar drops significantly, especially when hiking at high elevations or in extreme weather; this can be dangerous.

Energy bars are widely available in resupply towns and serve as great snacks. Some of my favorites include ProBars, Clif Bars, Luna Bars, date bars, fig bars, Sesame Snaps, Nature Valley granola bars, and Zing bars. Dried fruit and nuts are probably some of the most nutrient-dense snacks around.

Pro Tip: Many hikers eventually grow tired of eating sweet snacks, so salty foods like pretzels, corn chips, plantain chips, and dried chickpeas are great to combat flavor fatigue.

Dinner

Dinner is the time to focus more on protein. This meal should be a good balance of carbohydrates, protein, fat, and vegetables. The phytonutrients from vegetables and the amino acids from protein are key in promoting muscle recovery overnight. Eat as much as you possibly can for dinner, unless you plan to keep hiking. In that case, be sure to eat again before going to bed. As you rest, your body will be able to process all the nutrients you've given it and start to recover.

Resist the urge to snack right away when you reach camp (it's hard, I know), and save room for the most nutritious meal you'll have all day. Instead of a snack, I like to enjoy a hot cup of tea before dinner to help me rehydrate. If you choose to supplement your diet with a plant-based protein shake, after dinner or right before bed is a good time to have it. Again, this is a time when your body needs the protein to rebuild.

Pro Tip: Some things that always come in handy include flavor packets (miso packets, vegetarian gravy, taco seasoning, etc.) and dehydrated vegetables. With these two ingredients, you can make a meal out of almost anything. Add them to ramen, couscous, rice noodles, mashed potatoes, etc. to liven up the meal.

Junk Food

Sometimes you just need some chocolate and the only thing around is a pack of Oreos. Believe me, I've been there. Here is my perspective on vegan junk food.

First, make sure your diet is well balanced and covers all the bases: whole grains, legumes, fruits, vegetables, nuts, and seeds. If you're getting as much as possible of these food groups but still need more calories, there's nothing wrong with adding a little vegan junk food into the mix. If it'll make you happy, do it. Just make sure the majority of your calories come from whole, minimally processed foods.

The following is a list of lightweight, high-calorie vegan junk food that can be consumed in moderation:

- BelVita Breakfast Biscuits
- Fritos
- Oreos
- Pop Tarts (some unfrosted flavors)
- Potato chips
- Ramen (the Oriental and Chili flavors are vegan Top Ramen brand, but you can just leave out the flavor packets for any of them and use your own spices)
- Ritz Crackers
- Sour Patch Kids

- Teddy Grahams
- Triscuits

There are many more out there; these are just a few that come to mind.

Sample Meal Plans

DAY 1

	Food	Amount	Calories	Protein (g)
Break-fast	Granola with dried cherries	1 cup	300	7
	Mocha with powdered coconut milk, Starbucks Via, and Starbucks Double Chocolate hot cocoa mix	1 cup	200	5
Snack 1	Clif Bar (Chocolate Chip)	1	240	10
	Date bar (Larabar or similar)	1	220	7
Snack 2	Trail mix	½ cup	340	10
	Plantain chips	2 oz	280	0
Lunch	Oriental Flavor Top Ramen with dried veggies	1 package	380	10
	Added powdered peanut butter	2 tbsp	45	5
	Dried Mango	6 pieces	160	0
Snack 3	Peanut butter pretzels	11 pieces	140	5
	Luna Bar (Nutz over Chocolate)	1	200	9
Snack 4	ProBar (Chocolate Coconut)	1	370	8
	Candied walnuts	¼ cup	200	3
Dinner	Lentil stew with brown rice	1 ½ cups	375	24
	Added olive or coconut oil	1 tbsp	120	0
Snack 5	Dark chocolate	1 ounce	142	1
	Date bar (Larabar or similar)	1	200	5
Total			3,912 calories	109 grams protein

DAY 2

	Food	Amount	Calories	Protein (g)
Break-fast	Oatmeal with raisins, walnuts, brown sugar, chia and ground flax seeds	1 cup	200	5
	Coffee with 1 sugar packet	1 cup	20	0
Snack 1	Dried figs	1 cup	370	5
	Trail mix	½ cup	340	10
Snack 2	Clif Bar (Nut Butter Filled, Chocolate Peanut Butter)	1	230	7
	Dried cherries	¼ cup	130	1
Lunch	Potato soup	2 cups	255	15
	Added olive oil	1 tbsp	120	0
	Triscuits (Roasted Garlic)	2 ounces	240	6
Snack 3	Dried chickpeas (Biena brand)	¼ cup	120	6
	Luna Bar (Lemon Zest)	1	180	9
Snack 4	Dried bananas	2	260	4
	ProBar (Peanut Butter Chocolate Chip)	1	390	10
Dinner	Hot herbal tea with sugar packet	8 oz	20	0
	Curry with chickpeas and buckwheat noodles	2 cups	400	17
	Added peanut butter	2 tbsp	190	7
Snack 5	Dried mangoes	6	160	0
	Nature Valley granola bar (Pecan Crunch)	1	190	3
Total			3,815 calories	105 grams protein

DAY 3

	Food	Amount	Calories	Protein (g)
Break-fast	ProBar (Superfruit Slam)	1	350	8
	Hot Cocoa with coconut milk powder (Starbucks Double Chocolate Hot Cocoa packet	1 cup	270	4
Snack 1	Dried apricots	12	250	3
	Trail mix	½ cup	340	10
Snack 2	Clif Bar (Nuts and Seeds)	1	270	11
	Corn chips (Fritos Original)	2 ounces	320	0
Lunch	Tortillas with rehydrated hummus (add olive oil and water to rehydrate)	2 large tortillas, ½ cup hummus	360	14
	Peanut butter pretzels	11	140	5
Snack 3	Luna Bar (Nutz over Chocolate)	1	200	9
	Trail mix	½ cup	340	10
Snack 4	Triscuits	2 ounces	320	6
	Nature Valley granola bar (Pecan Crunch)	1	190	3
Dinner	Macaroni with cashew sauce and veggies	1 ½ cups	430	19
	Added olive oil	1 tbsp	120	0
Snack 5	Dried bananas	2	280	4
	Dark chocolate	1 ounce	142	1
Total			4,322 calories	107 grams protein

Chapter Five: Dehydrating Meals and Making Resupply Boxes

Thinking about planning meals for up to 5 months at a time can be an overwhelming task. It's best to start early and simply take one step at a time.

The first step in dehydrating backpacking meals is finding the right dehydrator. I recommend an Excalibur brand dehydrator. A four-tray Excalibur runs around $100 on Amazon (at the time of this writing). That being said, I have done plenty of dehydrating with whatever kind of dehydrator happens to be sitting in a friend's closet. A simple, round dehydrator is cheaper and will work just as well, though it is harder to remove the food from the tray because of the hole in the center. A jerky maker will also work, but you have to be careful since there is only one temperature setting (high). The ideal dehydrator has a timer and a knob to adjust temperature settings. It is also possible to dehydrate food in an oven set on a low temperature.

Next, choose a meal to make. It's a good idea to make big batches so that you maximize the number of meals you get at one time. Choose anything that looks good from the recipe chapters in this book, or adapt your favorite meal. The perfect dish for dehydrating has little to no added fat and can be mixed all together in one pot. The reason to avoid dehydrating fatty foods is that fat will not dehydrate. The meal will end up being greasy, and you run the risk of having the fats go rancid over time.

It is also helpful if you chop all the vegetables very finely. Small pieces dehydrate faster and are easier to rehydrate when you're on the trail. Thick, blended soups also dehydrate well.

When you spread your meal on dehydrator trays, make sure the plastic Teflex sheet is over each tray so that nothing falls through the cracks. Spread the meal relatively thinly on the sheet, then let it run for about 6–8 hours at a medium temperature. Check on the meal after 6–8 hours. If any part of it is not completely dry, let it run another couple of hours. You want to make sure the food is as dry as possible. Any wet food will go bad quickly. As long as the temperature is not too high, it's almost impossible to over-dehydrate. If the temperature is high, you risk eventually burning the meal.

After the food is dry, you may still need to chop up some meals into smaller pieces to facilitate easy rehydrating. Things like pasta, chickpeas, and big chunks of potatoes may need to be broken down further. Do this by putting the food in the blender a little bit at a time. Blend until the chunks are smaller but not until the entire meal is powder. You still want some texture left. This is time-consuming but worth it to avoid pieces of food that won't rehydrate well.

For short-term storage (1–3 months), a Ziploc bag is fine. For a longer period of storage (4 months to a year), seal the meals in Mylar with an oxygen absorber. You can find both of these items at Amazon. Use an iron or a hair straightener to seal the edges of the Mylar bag. Another option is to use a vacuum sealer, which is a bit more expensive but will guarantee freshness. If you have space in the refrigerator or freezer, store your meals there. Otherwise keep them in a cool, dark spot like an insulated garage until you are ready to send them in a resupply box.

Once you are on the trail, rehydrating your meal is the easy part. I find it best to add both the water and the dehydrated food to my cook pot, covering the food by about 1 inch with water. Bring the water to a boil, then let simmer for 1-3 minutes (depending on the amount of fuel you're willing to use up). Transfer your cook pot from the stove to a pot cozy to contain the heat, give it a quick stir with your spork, then let it sit for 10 minutes before enjoying.

If you don't want to dehydrate food

It's still possible, though perhaps not as enjoyable, to eat plant-based without making homemade meals. The following is a list of premade foods that are ideal for backpacking. Many can be found in the bulk aisle of a good grocery store.

- Dehydrated falafel
- Dehydrated hummus
- Earth Balance Mac and Cheese (many other brands of dairy-free mac and cheese are appearing on shelves these days, including Daiya and Amy's)
- Good To-Go meals
- Instant mashed potatoes (original flavor)
- Instant refried beans
- Mountain House Pad Thai
- Mountain House Louisiana Red Beans and Rice
- Near East couscous
- Outdoor Herbivore meals
- Taste Adventure: Instant Sweet Corn Chowder, Instant Split Pea Soup
- Top Ramen (Oriental and Chili Flavors, or eliminate flavor packet)

Assembling Resupply Boxes

After you spend a few months dehydrating meals and collecting many varieties of energy bars, dried nuts and fruit, powdered flavorings, hot chocolate, tea, and instant coffee, it's finally time to make sense of it all. I like to start with a spreadsheet where I calculate the number of miles and days between each town. From there, I put a sticky note on each box (I use priority flat-rate boxes) with the name of the town it goes to and how many days of food should be in it. Next, I distribute all the dinners according to how many days of food should be in each box. Then I distribute lunch and breakfast. Finally energy bars, salty snacks, dried fruit, coffee, tea, and any other essentials go in the boxes.

An average four-day resupply box might include the following:

- 4 dinners (about 1–2 cups of dried food per dinner)
- 2 cups of granola for breakfast
- 1 cup of oats for a different breakfast
- Instant coffee or tea bags
- Soy or coconut milk powder
- Hot cocoa powder
- At least 4 energy bars per day
- 2 cups of trail mix and/or salty snack

- 2 cups of dried fruit
- Peanut butter or hummus powder to put on tortillas (find tortillas in town)
- Instant soup mixes for lunch: split pea, corn chowder, miso, ramen
- 1 Ziploc bag of dried veggies
- Nutritional yeast and/or flavor packets
- A treat to eat right away: chocolate almond milk or a smoothie pouch

This has proven to be enough food for me, a female at 123 pounds. I have friends who eat less food than this and still have enough energy, while my hiking partner will eat about 50% more than this. Packing the right amount of food is a process of trial and error. More often than not, I end up with too much food, which is always better than not enough food.

Pro Tip: When planning resupply boxes for a hike lasting more than a few weeks, always plan for flavor fatigue! There's nothing worse than being stuck with the same nauseating food you've been eating for 3 months with no other options and no town for 50 miles. Variety is key.

Chapter Six: Eating in Towns

Breaks in town are ideal for loading up on as many calories as possible before heading back to the trail. But things get tricky when you wander into town hungry, tired, and hoping for something other than dehydrated curry. Hiker cravings are real, and for good reason. For many hikers, refueling in town is the only way to make sure that you get enough calories in the long run, since it is nearly impossible to carry enough calories with you on your back.

Depending on the town, it could be easy or hard to find plant-based options. Potatoes are usually widely available at any restaurant. Most places are willing to make a special meal using any combination of roasted potatoes, sautéed vegetables, fresh avocado, salsa, and a tortilla. Add some fresh fruit on the side, and you've got yourself a meal.

Other plant-based options include pizza joints and Mexican restaurants. A cheese-less pizza loaded with vegetables, substituting cashews for cheese, is a very satisfying option. Mexican restaurants often make vegetarian burritos that can be adapted to be vegan, and often have very large serving sizes. Some places even have veggie burgers available.

In towns with a good grocery store, there are endless options. You can easily buy a box of salad greens to mix with some avocado and fresh lime juice. Avocados are a great food to eat in town since they are both high in calories and in nutrients. Or find a loaf of bread to spread hummus on. If you have access to a microwave (maybe in your motel room), there may be a variety of frozen meals you can choose from. Be sure to pick up some fresh fruit while you're at the grocery store—and, if available, a pint of dairy-free ice cream. Time to load up on calories!

On the flip side, some towns have very dismal options. When you walk into the only restaurant within 50 miles and can't find a single vegetable on the menu, it's time to get creative. Make a meal out of French fries (and beer?), or wander over to the general store. You may be able to find some pasta and marinara sauce to cook on your camp stove, or a can of beans or soup to heat up.

Drawing the line

There comes a point where one must balance the need for calories with the desire to avoid animal products. Some people view the plant-based diet with an all-or-nothing approach. This eliminates the need to constantly make decisions about when to bend the rules and when not to. Knowing that you have clear boundaries of what you will and will not eat can make things much easier. This is a perfectly respectable approach. And, for most people, it is absolutely possible to remain 100 percent plant-based and still complete a thru-hike in a healthy way, despite the dismal food options in some towns.

Other people may need more flexibility. A thru-hike is not the ideal time to try to change your diet completely. A hiker should not feel restricted in any way when it comes to getting enough food. Allowing yourself to choose a grilled cheese sandwich when there is nothing else to eat is completely acceptable. It's better to eat *something* than to have nothing at all. However, this is an individual choice that will vary widely depending on the person.

Should you choose to stray from a plant-based diet at any point, keep in mind that certain foods, especially dairy and meat, may be very hard on your body to process if you haven't had them in a while. Be particularly careful if you are still planning on hiking more that day, as you don't want to end up on the side of the trail in a food-coma when you had intended to hike more miles.

Chapter Seven: Lunch/Dinner Recipes

Herby Lentil Stew

Lentils are the star of this easy one-pot meal. High in protein and fiber, they add a hearty, delicious texture to the soup. This is a great dinner for an evening when you plan to keep hiking, since lentils provide both protein and slow-burning carbohydrates. Lentil stew would taste great served over quinoa or brown rice.

Ingredients:
- 1 medium yellow onion, diced
- 4 cups vegetable broth, 2–4 tablespoons separated
- 3 cloves garlic, minced
- 1 cup green lentils
- 1 28-oz can diced or crushed tomatoes
- 1 ½ teaspoons smoked paprika
- 1 ½ teaspoons cumin
- 2 teaspoons marjoram
- 1 teaspoon thyme
- 1 teaspoon oregano
- 1 tablespoon maple syrup
- ¼ - ½ cup red wine (optional)
- 5 kale leaves, chopped
- Salt to taste

Preparation:

- Heat a large soup pot to medium heat. Add about 2 tablespoons of vegetable broth. When the broth starts to bubble, add onion.
- Sauté the onion in broth until translucent, adding more broth as needed to prevent the onion from sticking. Add the garlic and sauté for another minute.
- When the garlic is fragrant, add the remaining vegetable broth, tomatoes, lentils, paprika, and cumin. Bring to a boil, then reduce the heat and simmer for 30 minutes or until the lentils are soft.
- Add the herbs, maple syrup, red wine (if desired), and kale; stir to combine.
- Adjust the seasonings to taste.
- Optional step: use an immersion blender, or transfer to a blender, to blend into a smoother consistency. This may lead to easier rehydrating when the time comes.
- Enjoy some now, and/or let the rest cool to dehydrate. Spread the dish thinly on dehydrator sheets. Dehydrate on medium 6–10 hours until dry and crumbly.
- Divide the dry mixture into 1 or 2-cup portions, and place into resealable bags for storage.

Serves 4, Calories 259, Protein 24g, Fat 1g, Carb 36g, Fiber 6g

Bean and Sweet Potato Mash

This dish can be served either inside a tortilla or on its own, and is perfect for either lunch or dinner. Sweet potatoes and kale boost the antioxidant content for muscle recovery, while beans and rice provide sustained energy for more hiking.

Ingredients:
- 2 medium sweet potatoes, peeled and diced
- 1 bunch kale or other leafy green vegetable (collard, chard, spinach)
- 1 15-ounce can of black or pinto beans, drained and rinsed
- 1 15-ounce can of refried beans (vegetarian)
- 1 ½ cups frozen corn, thawed for 10 minutes
- 1 15-ounce jar of salsa
- 2 cups short grain brown rice, cooked
- Salt and pepper to taste

Preparation:
- Preheat the oven to 400 degrees Fahrenheit.
- Place the sweet potatoes on a nonstick or lightly greased pan, then bake them in the oven 20–30 minutes until you can stab them easily with a fork.
- Meanwhile, wash and chop the kale into bite-sized pieces.

- In a big pot or bowl, mix the beans, refried beans, corn, salsa, and rice.
- When the sweet potatoes are cooked through, remove them from the oven and place them in a bowl. Using a potato masher, mash them until only a few small chunks remain.
- Mix the sweet potatoes into the bean-and-rice mixture.
- Add the kale and salt and pepper to taste, and stir to combine.
- Enjoy some now, and/or get ready to dehydrate the rest. Spread the dish thinly on dehydrator sheets; it will spread more easily if it is still warm. Dehydrate on low overnight until all components are dry.
- Divide the dry mixture into 1 or 2-cup portions, and place into resealable bags for storage.

Serves 6, Calories 370, Protein 16g, Fat 3g, Carb 78g, Fiber 12g

Paul's Chickpea Curry

On my first complete thru-hike of the PCT, I ate this meal most frequently. My friend and fellow chef Paul Douglas served this in the kitchen where I was working for an event. Having overestimated the number of people who would be dining, we ended up with tons of leftover curry. At the end of the day, I came home with buckets of curry that I dehydrated. It was great to have something so hearty and delicious at the end of a long day of hiking.

Ingredients:
- 2–4 tablespoons vegetable broth
- 1 medium yellow onion, diced
- 2 large carrots, diced small
- 1 15-ounce can of light coconut milk
- 2 tablespoons red curry paste, plus more to taste
- 1 15-ounce can of diced tomatoes
- 1 15-ounce can of chickpeas, drained and rinsed
- 2 tablespoons tamari, plus more to taste
- 2 cups cooked brown rice, brown rice noodles, or buckwheat noodles for serving

Preparation:
- Add 2 tablespoons of vegetable broth to a medium saucepan over medium heat. When

the broth begins to bubble, add the onion and sauté until translucent. Then add the carrots and cook for 2 more minutes. Keep an eye on the pan, adding more broth as necessary so the contents don't stick.

- Mix in the coconut milk and red curry paste.
- Add the tomatoes, chickpeas, and tamari. Mix thoroughly and simmer until the carrots are soft and the sauce is thick enough to spread on a dehydrator sheet, about 5-10 minutes.
- Add more tamari and curry paste to taste. Serve over rice or noodles.
- Enjoy some now, and/or get ready to dehydrate the rest. You can dehydrate the dish with the rice/noodles mixed in or left out. Spread the dish thinly on dehydrator sheets. Dehydrate on low 8–12 hours until all components are dry.
- Divide the dry mixture into 1 or 2-cup portions, and place into resealable bags for storage.

Serves 5, Calories 288, Protein 9g, Fat 6g, Carb 46g, Fiber 8g

PCT Peanut Curry

The following recipe, like Paul's Chickpea Curry, is another basic curry recipe. As a hiker, you can never eat too much curry. The phytochemicals in curry spices like turmeric and cumin provide wonderful anti-inflammatory properties to help your muscles recover.

Ingredients:
- 1 cup cashews, soaked in 1 ½ cups of water for at least 2 hours
- 2–4 tablespoons vegetable broth
- 1 medium yellow onion, diced
- 1 medium red bell pepper, diced
- 2 tablespoons red curry paste, plus more to taste
- 2 tablespoons tamari, plus more to taste
- ¼ cup peanut butter
- 2 cups cooked brown rice, brown rice noodles, or buckwheat noodles for serving

Preparation:
- Without draining them, place cashews and water in a high speed blender. Blend until it reaches a smooth, creamy consistency, about 1-2 minutes, then set aside.
- Add 2 tablespoons of vegetable broth to a medium saucepan over medium heat. When

the broth begins to bubble, add the onion and sauté until translucent. Then add the bell pepper and cook for 2 more minutes. Add more broth as needed to prevent the vegetables from sticking to the pan.

- Mix in the cashew milk (blended cashews and water), red curry paste, tamari, and peanut butter. Mix thoroughly and simmer until the veggies are soft and the sauce is thick enough to spread on a dehydrator sheet, about 5-10 minutes.

- Add more tamari and curry paste to taste. Serve over rice or noodles.

- Enjoy some now, and/or get ready to dehydrate the rest. You can dehydrate the dish with the rice/noodles mixed in or left out. Spread the dish thinly on dehydrator sheets. Dehydrate on low 8–12 hours until all components are dry.

- Divide the dry mixture into 1-cup or 2-cup portions, and place into resealable bags for storage.

*Note: A high-speed blender is not required. Soak the cashews overnight for best results if using a regular blender or food processor. The longer the cashews soak, the creamier the result.

Serves 5, Calories 318, Protein 11g, Fat 16g, Carb 32g, Fiber 4g

Potato Leek Soup

This is my hiking partner Mud's favorite lunch. It's simple, flavorful, and full of great nutrients. The combination of potatoes and nutritional yeast gives this a nice texture reminiscent of a cream-based soup, but better!

Ingredients:
- 4 cups plus 2–4 tablespoons vegetable broth
- 1 large leek, chopped, green parts removed
- 3 medium Yukon Gold potatoes, peeled and cubed
- 1 cup nondairy milk of choice (almond, soy, coconut)
- ¼ cup nutritional yeast
- ¼ teaspoon salt, plus more to taste
- ½ teaspoon pepper, plus more to taste

Preparation:
- Add 2 tablespoons of vegetable broth to a large stockpot, heat to medium-high. Once broth starts to bubble, add the leek. Sauté for 6-8 minutes until the leek starts to soften and brown. Add more vegetable broth as needed to prevent the leek from sticking.
- Add the potatoes, 2 cups of vegetable broth, and the nondairy milk. Simmer for 30–40 minutes until the potatoes are tender. Be

careful; this soup tends to splatter and spit when it gets too hot on the stove!

- Add the nutritional yeast, salt, and pepper.
- Ladle the soup mixture into a blender, or blend it in the pot with an immersion blender. Blend until a creamy consistency is reached.
- Adjust the seasonings according to taste.
- Enjoy some now, and/or get ready to dehydrate the rest. The soup should be thick enough to spread on a dehydrator sheet without running over the edges. You may want to thin some out if you're eating it right away. Spread the soup thinly on dehydrator sheets, and dehydrate on low 8–10 hours.
- Divide the dry mixture into 1 or 2-cup portions, and place into resealable bags for storage.

Serves 4, Calories 255, Protein 15g, Fat 1g, Carb 38g, Fiber 5g

Creamy Broccoli Soup

Broccoli is actually one of the higher-protein vegetables. As a cruciferous vegetable, it also has powerful cancer-fighting properties. This soup is another delicious, creamy way to get more vegetables during your hike. Eat this for lunch or dinner—it goes great with crackers!

Ingredients:
- 2–4 tablespoons vegetable broth or water
- 1 medium yellow onion, diced
- 3 cloves garlic, chopped
- 4 cups vegetable broth
- 3 medium Yukon Gold potatoes, roughly chopped and peeled
- 2 heads of broccoli, roughly chopped
- 1 tablespoon olive oil
- 1 tablespoon lemon juice
- 1 tablespoon white miso
- ¼ cup nutritional yeast, plus more to taste
- 2 tablespoons tahini
- Salt and pepper to taste

Preparation:
- Preheat the oven to 400 degrees Fahrenheit.
- In a large stockpot, heat 2 tablespoons of vegetable broth or water on medium-high heat. When the liquid begins to bubble, add the onion and garlic. Cook for 2 minutes or

until the onions are translucent. Add more broth/water as needed to prevent sticking.

- Add 4 cups of vegetable broth and the potatoes. Bring to a boil, then reduce the heat and simmer for 15 minutes.
- Place the broccoli in a nonstick baking pan, and toss with olive oil and salt. Place in the oven and cook for 15 minutes or until slightly crispy on the edges.
- When the broccoli is cooked and the potatoes are tender, add the broccoli, lemon juice, miso, nutritional yeast, and tahini to the pot and stir to combine.
- Ladle the soup mixture into a blender, or blend it in the pot with an immersion blender. Blend until a creamy consistency is reached.
- Add more nutritional yeast for a cheesier flavor and salt and pepper to taste, then transfer the mixture back to the pot. Adjust the seasonings accordingly.
- Enjoy some now, and/or get ready to dehydrate the rest. Spread the dish thinly on dehydrator sheets, and dehydrate on low 8–10 hours.
- When the soup is dry, crumble it into small pieces using your hands or a blender. Divide the dry mixture into 1 or 2-cup portions, and place into resealable bags for storage.

Serves 5, Calories 315, Protein 27g, Fat, 8g, Carb 44g, Fiber 13g

Bug's Macaroni and Sauce

There are many variations of the classic macaroni and cheese. Some of my favorites include using butternut squash or cashews as a creamy base for the sauce. In this recipe, I use both. For a truly decadent meal, add some Field Roast sausage (chopped small for optimal dehydrating) for an extra protein kick.

Ingredients:
- 1 small butternut squash or 2 cups frozen cubed butternut squash (thawed)
- ½ cup cashews, soaked for 2 hours in 1 cup of water
- ¼ cup nutritional yeast
- ¼ teaspoon nutmeg
- 2 teaspoons onion powder
- 2 teaspoons garlic powder
- ½ teaspoon turmeric
- ½ teaspoon paprika
- ¼ teaspoon crushed red pepper flakes
- 1 tablespoon tamari
- 3 cups Brussels sprouts, finely chopped
- 1 tablespoon olive oil
- Salt and pepper to taste
- 1 pound of ditali lisci pasta or small macaroni

Preparation:
- Preheat the oven to 400 degrees Fahrenheit. Cut the butternut squash in half, and scoop out the seeds with a spoon. Place the halves on an ungreased baking sheet and bake 1 hour or until tender. If using precut cubes, roast in a nonstick pan or parchment-paper lined baking sheet for 30 minutes or until crispy around the edges. Remove and let cool.
- When the squash is cool, scoop out the flesh into a blender or food processor. Add the soaked cashews with their water, nutritional yeast, and all remaining seasonings. Blend until smooth, adding more water as needed.
- Spread the Brussels sprouts on a baking sheet and toss with the olive oil, salt, and pepper. Bake for 30 minutes or until slightly browned and crisp.
- While the sprouts are baking, set a large pot of water to boil and cook the pasta according to the directions on the package.
- When everything is cooked, place the squash mixture, sprouts, and pasta in a large bowl, and stir to combine.
- Enjoy some now, and/or get ready to dehydrate the rest. Spread the dish thinly on dehydrator sheets, and dehydrate on low 8–10 hours.

- Divide the dry mixture into 1 or 2-cup portions, and place into resealable bags for storage.

Serves 6, Calories 431, Protein 19g, Fat 9g, Carb 72, Fiber 9g

Mexican Couscous Salad

This salad is a great, refreshing meal on a warm day. You can rehydrate it over the stove or cold-hydrate it in the morning to be ready for a wholesome lunch. Just put the couscous with water in a sealed container (like an empty peanut butter jar or a pot with a lid) in the morning, wait a few hours, and enjoy!

Ingredients:
- ¾ cup water
- 1 pinch salt
- ½ cup Israeli couscous (also called pearl couscous)
- ½ medium red onion, finely diced
- 1 15-ounce can of black beans
- 2 cups frozen corn
- 1 red bell pepper, chopped
- 1 bunch cilantro, chopped
- ¼ cup lime juice
- 1 tablespoon taco seasoning

Preparation:
- In a small saucepan, bring the water to a boil with a pinch of salt. When the water is boiling, add the couscous. Cover and reduce the heat to low. Simmer for 10 minutes or until the

water is absorbed. Uncover and cool for 3 minutes before fluffing with a fork.

- In a medium bowl, combine all other ingredients. Add the couscous when it is cool. Mix well to combine.
- Enjoy some now, and/or get ready to dehydrate the rest. Spread the dish thinly on dehydrator sheets, and dehydrate on low 8–10 hours until all components are dry.
- Divide the dry mixture into 1 or 2-cup portions, and place into resealable bags for storage.

Serves 5, Calories 286, Protein 13g, Fat 2g, Carbohydrate 60g, Fiber 7g

Quinoa Sweet Potato Medley

Quinoa and beans make this dish very high in protein. Quinoa rehydrates well and is a good alternative to rice on the trail. The addition of lime juice makes this a very light and refreshing meal. This recipe is adapted from and inspired by one of my favorite bloggers, Cathy Fisher. You can find more meals like this on her website, www.straightupfood.com.

Ingredients:
- 2 medium sweet potatoes, peeled and cubed
- 2 cups plus 2 tablespoons water
- 1 cup uncooked quinoa
- 1 small yellow onion, diced
- 3–4 cloves garlic, minced
- 1 bunch collard greens, chopped
- 1 15-ounce can of pinto or black beans
- ½ bunch cilantro, chopped
- ½ cup lime juice
- 1 ½ teaspoons cumin
- 1 teaspoon smoked paprika
- 1 teaspoon chili powder
- Salt and pepper to taste
- Sliced avocado for serving

Preparation:

- Preheat the oven to 350 degrees Fahrenheit. Place the sweet potato cubes on a lightly greased or nonstick baking sheet, and bake 20–30 minutes or until they are crisp on the outside and soft on the inside.
- Meanwhile, add 2 cups water and the quinoa to a medium saucepan. Cover, bring to a boil, then reduce the heat and simmer for 20 minutes or until the water is absorbed. Cool for 10 minutes.
- In a different pan, sauté the onion in 2 tablespoons of water on medium heat until translucent. Add the garlic and greens, adding more water as needed. Cook until all vegetables are soft.
- After the sweet potatoes and quinoa have cooked, mix the sweet potatoes, quinoa, vegetables, beans, cilantro, lime juice, and seasonings in a medium bowl.
- If you're enjoying the dish right away, top with some sliced avocado and dig in! If you're dehydrating, spread the dish thinly on dehydrator sheets and dehydrate on low 8–10 hours.
- Divide the dry mixture into 1 or 2-cup portions, and place into resealable bags for storage.

Serves 5, Calories 327, Protein 11g, Fat 8g, Carbs 57, Fiber 12g

Chapter Eight: Breakfast and Other Recipes

Mom's Granola

I'm lucky enough to have a mom who mails me fresh, homemade granola while I'm thru-hiking. But you can always make your own and send it ahead! Granola is a great, high-calorie breakfast and a powerhouse of nutrients. This is my mom's recipe and one of the most simple and delicious that I have found.

Ingredients:
- 4 cups rolled oats
- 1 ½ cups of nuts (for example, ½ cup almond slices, ½ cup walnuts, and ½ cup pecans)
- ½ cup wheat germ or ground flaxseed
- ½ cup sunflower seeds
- ½ teaspoon salt
- ¼ cup oil (coconut, sunflower, or canola)
- ½ cup maple syrup
- 1 teaspoon vanilla
- 1 cup dried cranberries or raisins

Preparation:
- Preheat the oven to 350 degrees Fahrenheit.
- Mix all ingredients together except the cranberries or raisins.
- Spread the mixture thinly on 2 ungreased baking sheets.

- Bake for 30 minutes, stirring every 10 minutes.
- Let the granola cool, then add the cranberries or raisins.

Serves 15, Calories 313, Protein 7g, Fat 18g, Carb 34g, Fiber 5g

Banana Bread Pudding

Bananas, sweet potatoes, and oats are a powerful combination and a great way to start the day with plenty of complex carbohydrates for slow-burning energy. This pudding is best rehydrated hot, as cold hydration may leave it a bit chunky.

Ingredients:
- 2 medium sweet potatoes
- ½ cup rolled oats
- 1 ripe banana, peeled
- ½ cup nondairy milk of choice (such as almond, soy, or coconut)
- 1 teaspoon lemon juice
- 1 tablespoon maple syrup
- 1 teaspoon cinnamon
- ½ teaspoon vanilla
- ¼ teaspoon salt

Preparation:
- Preheat the oven to 350 degrees Fahrenheit. Poke a few holes in the sweet potatoes with a fork, and place them on a baking sheet lined with aluminum foil. Bake for 1 hour until the sweet potatoes are tender, then cool for 30 minutes.
- When the sweet potatoes are cool, peel off the skin and add them to a food processor.

- Add all other ingredients. Process until smooth, about 2 minutes.
- Spread the mixture thinly on dehydrator sheets, and dehydrate on low for 8–12 hours until dry and pliable.
- For optimal rehydrating, put the dried pudding into a blender and mix until the pieces are very small. Doing so will allow the pudding to rehydrate faster.
- Divide the dry mixture into 1 or 2-cup portions, and place into resealable bags for storage.

Serves 4, Calories 149, Protein 4g, Fat 2g, Carb 31g, Fiber 4g

Standard Sweet Potato Mash

This dish is great to have on hand as a breakfast option or just to add to other meals as needed. It's easy to get sick of oatmeal, so having sweet potato mash in the morning offers much needed variety. It also goes well added to any meal of beans and rice.

Ingredients:
- 2 medium sweet potatoes
- 1 tablespoon maple syrup (optional)
- ¼ teaspoon salt

Preparation:
- Preheat the oven to 400 degrees Fahrenheit. Poke holes in the sweet potatoes with a fork, and place them on baking sheet lined with aluminum foil. Bake for 1 hour until the sweet potatoes are tender, remove from oven, then let cool for 30 minutes.
- When the sweet potatoes are cool, peel off the skin.
- In a medium bowl, use a potato masher to mix the sweet potatoes with maple syrup, if using, and salt. Mash until the consistency is smooth.
- Spread the mixture thinly on a dehydrator sheet. Dehydrate on low 8–10 hours.
- When the bark is dehydrated, make sure to crunch it up into small pieces for optimal

rehydration. Do this using your hands or a blender.

- Divide the dry mixture into 1-cup or 2-cup portions, and place into resealable bags for storage.

Serves 2, Calories 138, Protein 2g, Fat 0g, Carbs 33g, Fiber 4g

Raw Zucchini Chips

This recipe comes from two of my best hiker-friends, Harpo and Groucho (www.wrongwaygang.com). The zucchini chips are light and crispy. They dehydrate better without oil—salting the zucchini first and sweating it for a few minutes helps bind the yeast. Although they're not super calorie-dense, they are tasty and quite easy to prepare. They also make an awesome vehicle for hummus or refried beans and are good crumbled on soup.

Ingredients:
- 3 large zucchini
- ½ teaspoon coarse sea salt
- 1/2 cup nutritional yeast
- 1 ½ teaspoons smoked paprika (optional)
- 1 ½ teaspoons garlic powder (optional)
- Fresh ground black pepper to taste

Preparation:
- Thinly slice the zucchini using either a mandolin or chef's knife, then place slices in a large bowl.
- Toss the zucchini with salt and let sit for 3-5 minutes.
- Add the nutritional yeast, salt, and pepper. Add smoked paprika and garlic powder if desired. Mix with your hands or a wooden spoon.

- Place the zucchini slices in single layers on dehydrator trays. Dehydrate on 105 degrees (F) for about 8–12 hours, depending on the thickness of the slices.
- When the chips are dry, divide them into 1-cup or 2-cup portions, and place in resealable bags for storage.

Serves 10, Calories 81, Protein 10g, Fat 0g, Carbs 10g, Fiber 4g

Dehydrated Vegetables

It's always good to have some vegetables on hand in your food bag. Add them to ramen, couscous, mashed potatoes, or any meal that needs a little extra nutrition and flavor. The following is just a suggestion of vegetables. Of course, you can apply this to any vegetable you choose.

Ingredients:
- 2–4 tablespoons water
- Onions (red, yellow, or white)
- Carrots
- Cabbage (green or purple)
- Broccoli

Preparation:
- Chop all vegetables as finely as possible.
- Heat the water in a large saucepan on medium heat. Add the onions and cook until translucent, adding more water as needed to prevent them from sticking.
- Add the rest of the vegetables and cook until brightly colored, 5–10 minutes.
- Remove the vegetables from the pan and spread them on a dehydrator sheet. Dehydrate on low 8–10 hours until all vegetables are dry.

- Divide the dry mixture into 1-cup or 2-cup portions, and place into resealable bags for storage

Nutrition information will vary based on amount of vegetables.

Trail Ramen

Ramen is the ultimate thru-hiker food. You can find it almost anywhere for less than a dollar. It's cheap, lightweight, and high in calories. Unfortunately, it is also almost completely devoid of nutrients. By adding peanut butter and veggies, you can elevate your ramen into a fairly complete meal.

Ingredients:
- 1 3-oz package ramen, flavor packet removed
- ½ 3-oz package of miso soup flavoring
- 2 tablespoons dehydrated vegetables (see preceding recipe)
- 1 tablespoon powdered or regular peanut butter (optional)
- 1 package Sriracha or hot sauce (about 2 teaspoons)

Preparation:
- Mix all ingredients together in an empty peanut butter jar or a Ziploc freezer bag.
- Add enough water to cover the ingredients by at least ½ inch. Mix well.
- Place the dish in your pack and hike 1–3 hours before enjoying.
- For a warm meal, add all ingredients to 1 ½ cups of boiling water and stir. Dig in after 3–5 minutes of soaking.

Serves 1, Calories 475, Protein 15g, Fat 16g, Carbs 68g, Fiber 5g

Mud's Morning Oatmeal

My hiking partner Mud's secret trail name is Oatmeal. Not only does he eat oatmeal for breakfast, but he also might have it at any point throughout the day, and especially as a bedtime snack. Using rolled oats instead of instant and adding chia seeds and flaxseeds help increase the fiber and keep you full for longer. The chia seeds, flaxseeds, and walnuts also serve as an important source of anti-inflammatory omega-3 fats.

Ingredients:
- 1 cup water
- ½ cup rolled oats
- 1 tablespoon flaxseeds, chia seeds, or Barlean's flax/chia/coconut blend
- 1 tablespoon brown sugar
- 2 tablespoons dried cranberries or cherries, or to taste
- 2 tablespoons walnuts, or to taste

Preparation:
- Bring the water to a boil and add the oats, seeds, and brown sugar.
- Depending how mushy you like your oatmeal, either let the oatmeal simmer 1–2 minutes (for a mushy texture), or turn off the stove and let

it soak 3–5 minutes (for a less mushy texture and to conserve fuel).
- When the oats are cooked, add cranberries and walnuts to taste. Enjoy!

Serves 1, Calories 313, Protein 8g, Fat 11g, Carbs 50g, Fiber 8g

Bug's Mocha

This mocha is the perfect midmorning pick-me-up after getting up before dawn to crush miles. You can buy powdered coconut milk at most health food stores, sold by a brand called Native Forest. If coconut milk is unavailable, powdered soy milk is an acceptable replacement.

Ingredients:
- 1 cup water
- 1 packet of Starbucks Via instant coffee
- 1.5 tablespoons powdered coconut milk (to taste)
- 2 tablespoons nondairy powdered hot cocoa mix like Starbucks Double Chocolate Hot Cocoa Mix (to taste)

Preparation:
- Bring the water to a boil.
- Mix all the powdered ingredients together in a cup.
- Add the water to the powdered ingredients, stir, and enjoy!

Serves 1, Calories 200, Protein 5g, Fat 11g, Carbs 26g, Fiber 3g

Hobo Salad

This salad is a great way to get in fresh, leafy green vegetables while you're in town. Of course, there are multiple variations—get creative with whatever you can find in the grocery store! If you can't finish a whole box of salad greens by yourself, it's always a good idea to find a friend and share the wealth.

Ingredients:
- 1 medium avocado
- 1 medium lime
- 1 5-oz box of salad greens
- 1 jar of salsa, any size (if you can find the kind with beans, choose that one)
- 1 bag of tortilla chips, any size
- 1 15-oz can of black beans (optional; if you can find a can opener or a can with a pull tab)

Preparation:
- Slice both the avocado and lime in half; these will serve as the salad dressing.
- Squeeze the avocado meat out on top of the greens, then juice the lime on top of the greens. Massage both into the leaves.
- Top with a few scoops of salsa and crumbled tortillas. Add some beans, if using.
- Dig in with your spork and enjoy!

Serves 4, Calories 262, Protein 8g, Fat 11g, Carbs 37g, Fiber 10g

Don't Go Yet!

If you enjoyed this book, you may be interested in checking out my blog! At the website NourishingJourneyPCT.com, you can find more tips for thru-hiking on a plant-based diet, contact me for a personal nutrition consult, as well as keep up with my adventures. I have also posted a spreadsheet, made in collaboration with three other vegan thru-hikers, regarding resupply towns along the PCT. It details what you can expect to find in terms of plant-based options in each town and may be very helpful in planning your trip.

If you liked this guide, I would be so happy if you'd wander over to Amazon and leave an honest review on the book's page. The more reviews it has, the more easily others will be able to find it, thanks to Amazon's internal algorithm calculations. Thank you!

About the Author

Anna Herby, MS, RD, grew up in the Appalachian Mountains of Virginia where her family instilled in her an unwavering love and appreciation for the natural world. She spent summers hiking through the Shenandoah mountain range, leading backpacking trips as a counselor at Shiloh Quaker Camp. The feeling of freedom, complete exhaustion and connection with the earth that she found during these trips served as a guide for subsequent life choices.

She went on to earn a Masters of Science in Nutrition at Bastyr University. It was during her time at Bastyr in Seattle, Washington that she first set foot on the Pacific Crest Trail. Since then, she's completed over four thousand miles of thru-hiking. Anna has learned from some of the best in plant-based nutrition, completing internships with the Physician's Committee for Responsible Medicine in Washington DC and the McDougall Program in Santa Rosa, CA. She worked as a facilitator for the Complete Health Improvement Program in Walla Walla, Washington, giving cooking demonstrations and helping patients transition to a plant-based lifestyle. Currently, she works as a Registered Dietitian, Diabetes Specialist, in Okanogan, WA, helping individuals to overcome chronic disease through dietary changes.

Acknowledgements

Thank you to all those who have cheered me on along this journey and continue to do so. To Erika and Sarah for testing recipes; Georgette, Erika, Mud and my mom for editing; to Laura for the marketing tips; and to Christina for the wonderful cover design. And to all the outdoor enthusiasts, just like me, who want to change the world, one meal at a time. Thank you for your support!

References

1. Balke B, Snow C. Anthropological and physiological observations on Tarahumara endurance runners. *Am J Phys Anthropol.* 1965;23(3):293–301. doi:10.1002/ajpa.1330230317.
2. Acosta Navarro JC, Cárdenas Prado SM, Cárdenas PA, Santos RD, Caramelli B. Pre-historic eating patterns in Latin America and protective effects of plant-based diets on cardiovascular risk factors. *Clinics.* 2010;65(10):1049–1054. doi:10.1590/S1807-59322010001000022.
3. Cerqueira MT, Fry MM, Connor WE. The food and nutrient intakes of the Tarahumara Indians of Mexico. *Am J Clin Nutr.* 1979;32:905–915.
4. McAnulty LS, Nieman DC, Dumke CL, Shooter LA, Henson DA, Utter AC, Milne G, McAnulty SR. Effect of blueberry ingestion on natural killer cell counts, oxidative stress, and inflammation prior to and after 2.5 h of running. *Appl Physiol Nutr Metab.* 2011;36(6):976–984. doi: 10.1139/h11-120.
5. Kuehl KS, Perrier ET, Elliot DL, Chesnutt JC. Efficacy of tart cherry juice in reducing muscle pain during running: a randomized controlled trial. *J Int Soc Sports Nutr.* 2010;7:17. doi:10.1186/1550-2783-7-17.
6. Turner-McGrievy GM, Wirth MD, Shivappa N, Wingard EE, Fayad R, Wilcox, S, et al. Randomization to plant-based dietary approaches leads to larger short-term improvements in Dietary Inflammatory Index scores and macronutrient intake compared with diets that contain meat. *Nutr Res.* 2015;35(2):97–106.
7. Morimoto Y, Beckford F, Cooney RV, Franke AA, Maskarinec G. Adherence to cancer prevention recommendations and antioxidant and inflammatory status in premenopausal women. *Br J Nutr.* 2015;114(1):134–143. doi:10.1017/S0007114515001658.
8. Adam O, Beringer C, Kless T, Lemmen C, Adam A, Wiseman M, et al. Anti-inflammatory effects of a low arachidonic acid diet and fish oil in patients with rheumatoid arthritis. *Rheumatol Int.* 2003;23(1):27–36. Epub 2002 Sep 6.
9. Watzl B. Anti-inflammatory effects of plant-based foods and of their constituents. *Int J Vitam Nutr Res.* 2008;78(6):293–298.

10. Campbell TC, Campbell TM. *The China Study: The Most Comprehensive Study of Nutrition Ever Conducted and the Startling Implications for Diet, Weight Loss, and Long-term Health.* Dallas, TX: BenBella; 2005.
11. Greger M. Dr. Burkitt's F-Word Diet. http://nutritionfacts.org/video/dr-burkitts-f-word-diet/.
12. Young VR, Pellett PL. Plant proteins in relation to human protein and amino acid nutrition. *Am J Clin Nutr.* 1994;59(5 Suppl):1203S–1212S.
13. Greger M. The Protein-Combining Myth. https://nutritionfacts.org/video/the protein-combining-myth/.
14. Campbell TC. The Mystique of Protein and Its Implications. http://nutritionstudies.org/mystique-of-protein-implications/.
15. McDougall J. When Friends Ask: Where Do You Get Your Protein? April 2007 Newsletter. http://www.drmcdougall.com/misc/2007nl/apr/protein.htm.
16. Wang DD, Li Y, Chiuve SE, et al. Association of specific dietary fats with total and cause-specific mortality. *JAMA Intern Med.* Published online July 5, 2016.
17. Rizos EC, Ntzani EE, Bika E, Kostapanos MS. Association between omega-3 fatty acid supplementation and risk of major cardiovascular disease events: a systematic review and meta-analysis. *JAMA* 2012;308:1024-1033
18. Zhao SP, Liu L, Gao M, Zhou QC, Li YL, Xia B. Impairment of endothelial function after a high-fat meal in patients with coronary artery disease. *Coron Artery Dis.* 2001 Nov;12(7):561-5.
19. Lundman P, Eriksson M, Schenck-Gustafsson K, Karpe F, Tornvall P. Transient triglyceridemia decreases vascular reactivity in young, healthy men without risk factors for coronary heart disease. *Circulation.* 1997 Nov 18;96(10):3266-8.
20. Crowe KM, Francis C. 2013. Position of the academy of nutrition and dietetics: functional foods. *Journal of the Academy of Nutrition and Dietetics*, 113(8), pp. 1096-1103.
21. Appleby, P. et all (2007). Comparative fracture risk in vegetarians and nonvegetarians in EPIC-Oxford, *European Journal of Clinical Nutrition*, Vol 61 No 12, pages 1400-6.

22. Michaelsson K, Wolk A, Langenskiold S, et al. Milk intake and risk of mortality and fractures in women and men: cohort studies. *BMJ* 2014 Oct 28;349:g6015.

Made in the USA
Columbia, SC
22 May 2020